A Life with Animals

A photographic celebration
of The Aspinall Foundation
and family

Published by The Aspinall Foundation.
www.aspinallfoundation.org
Email: info@aspinallfoundation.org

First published 2014.
Copyright © The Aspinall Foundation, 2014.
All rights reserved.

The moral right of the author has been asserted.

Printed by Cliffe Enterprises.
Written and edited by Lisa Mendes, designed by John Devlin at The Design Practice.
Project manager: Chris Gray.

ISBN: 978-0-9930038-06.

Every effort has been made to contact copyright owners of the material enclosed. Anyone who has not been contacted for any reason is requested to write to the publishers so that full credit can be made in subsequent editions.

contents

foreword

Thirty years ago, my father, the late John Aspinall, founded The Aspinall Foundation of which I am now proudly Chairman. Spurred on by what he saw as the rampant destruction of surviving wildlife habitats around the world, he decided to form a not-for-profit organisation that would do everything in its power to protect the world's rare and endangered species from the threat of extinction through a combination of ground-breaking breeding and reintroduction programmes, both in the UK and abroad.

Today, thanks to his vision and the hard work, generosity and cooperation of family members, patrons, governments and dedicated conservationists, The Aspinall Foundation (TAF) has managed to achieve a healthy record of successes in this regard. Not only is it world-renowned for its breeding programmes of rare and endangered animal species, but over the years, it has managed to successfully reintroduce gorillas, European bison, black rhino, Javan langurs, Javan gibbons, and Przewalski horses; as well as repatriate ocelots and clouded leopards to sanctuaries in their native habitats.

Taking my father's work forward, we continue to focus on how to improve and expand on our current conservation and reintroduction programmes around the world, as well as act to curb illegal wildlife trafficking and protect areas rich in natural biodiversity, in the hope that one day we can remove more animals from the critically endangered species' lists.

Along The Aspinall Foundation's three decade-long journey, which has had its share of highs and lows, we have managed to amass some wonderful memories, many of which have been documented through the medium of film and photography. This includes one of our most recent success stories: the moving and gratifying account of Djala the gorilla's return to the wilds of Africa over 2013-14.

At this juncture in the charity's history, we thought it might be nice to share some of these memories with you, both to acknowledge what we have accomplished thus far, and also as a way of saying thank you to all the many people (and animals) who have helped to make this possible.

I hope you will enjoy commemorating these achievements with us. We are now looking forward to the next thirty years, celebrating more memorable moments and conservation milestones for our planet in the future.

Damian Aspinall
2014

introduction

On the 29th of April 2014, The Aspinall Foundation turned 30. The charity has its founder, the visionary and charismatic John Aspinall, to thank for both its name and ambitious conservation aims, both of which continue to be driven forward in the person of Damian Aspinall, John's eldest son and current TAF Chairman.

From a very young age, John Aspinall had a fascination with animals, revelling in the company of his relatives' exotic animals as a child in India, and then later as a schoolboy in England, keeping a succession of unusual creatures of his own, including a ferret and several jackdaws; and eagerly learning about animal husbandry at the Sussex farm where he spent his summer holidays.

However, it was a rather sorry and forlorn monkey which his first wife, Jane, took pity on and insisted he buy one day in Harrods that served as the catalyst for what would become a life-long obsession with rescuing and protecting wild animals. The creature in question was a capuchin monkey that John named 'Dead Loss,' mainly because he didn't expect it to live terribly long, given its no doubt difficult and sad life within the exotic animals trade up until that point. Defying all the odds, though, 'Dheddi,' as he became known, thrived under the couple's care, living to the ripe old age of around 35! He was soon joined by a tigress called Tara and a pair of Himalayan bears, Esau and Ayesha.

The need to better house this growing menagerie of animals, most of whom were clearly not cut out for life in a London maisonette, spurred John into buying what is now a 100-acre estate in Bekesbourne near Canterbury, Kent. True to form, he paid for Howletts with a large win at the horses and the rest, as they say, is history. What started out as a personal hobby soon turned into a burning passion for animal rights and wildlife conservation, leading eventually to the establishment of The Aspinall Foundation (TAF) in 1984.

From the beginning, the organisation had a family feel about it, no doubt in large part because many of its original trustees and animal caretakers were part of the Aspinall clan. Another big contributing factor was John's deep bonds with the animals in his care, most of whom he viewed as close friends – a gift he passed on to his son Damian. Unlike many other zoo-keepers of his day, though, John was somewhat unique in placing the happiness and welfare of his animals above that of commercial concerns, and was not afraid to try new things, even if this came at great personal cost or vociferous criticism from naysayers.

Ultimately, though, his foresight, determination and willingness to take risks paid off. Today, both Howletts and Port Lympne boast unrivalled breeding records, and The Aspinall Foundation has achieved some remarkable feats in its three decade-long existence.

With so much to celebrate, it seemed fitting to mark the occasion with a book of photos selected from The Aspinall Foundation 'family' photo album. Many of these were taken by Dave Rolfe, the resident parks photographer, who has been documenting the work of the charity and its parks for the last 27 years. During this time, he has witnessed everything from rare animal births and new species arrivals to the return of several waves of captive-born animals over the decades.

We hope you enjoy taking this journey through The Aspinall Foundation archives, and thank you for helping us get to this important point in our history.

the passion of a family

At its heart, The Aspinall Foundation (or TAF for short) has always been about friends and family: the charity has its roots in the passion of a family that has devoted their lives to the care and protection of wild animals, many of whom they consider to be their friends.

John Aspinall was exceptional for his time because he viewed animals as equals, if not as superior to most human beings, and went to great lengths to cultivate a bond of love and trust with them.

No doubt as a result of his father's personal passion and early encounters with wildlife, Damian Aspinall and his siblings also developed strong bonds with animals from an early age. Amanda, Damian's sister, adopted and raised a wild boar called 'Yiddle' when she was just eleven; while his mother Jane, and two stepmothers, Min and Sally, along with his grandmothers, Lady Osborne and Dorothy Hastings, all took turns to raise a litany of orphaned or abandoned animals over the years.

Some of Damian's closest childhood companions were gorillas, and he recalls many a fond memory of his youth:

"(I had) an extraordinarily blessed childhood. We've got Super 8 films from the 60s of me as a seven-year-old, playing with tigers and bison around a tree or tearing around the lawns with a gang of wolves; and all of us being chased and diving in the pond to try to get away from the wasps after we upset their nest."

In keeping with the family tradition, Damian has passed on this love and respect for nature to his children Tansy, Clary and Freya, who like to get involved with TAF projects and help out or interact with the animals whenever possible.

In their quest to secure the future of the world's most threatened species, the Aspinalls have been joined by an extended circle of like-minded individuals, all of whom have helped to contribute to the successes of TAF since its inception in 1984. The list of illustrious park visitors and TAF supporters over the years has ranged from politicians and artists, to celebrities and even royalty.

"Respect is the secret ingredient that enables a mere human to cross the threshold into nature's realm." JOHN ASPINALL

John Aspinall with Assam, an Indian bull elephant from his troupe at Port Lympne. The eldest of the group, Assam was born on Valentine's Day 1968 in Hanover Zoo, Germany, according to John. The first Indian elephant to be acquired for Howletts, he arrived in spring 1971 and was soon followed by another bull and two cows, all rescued from a life of servitude as beasts of burden from an elephant market in Bihar, India. Sadly, although several attempts were made to breed with him, both his offspring either died in infancy or were stillborn. The whole troupe was later transferred to Port Lympne in 1977 where they enjoyed six acres of grassland in which to roam – more than any other zoo at the time.

Damian Aspinall playing with some gorilla babies. A product of the TAF breeding programmes, they were given a new home in a conservation area bordering the Congo and Gabon where The Aspinall Foundation has set up a gorilla rehabilitation project within a protected reserve on the Batéke Plateau. This group was a follow up to the first successful reintroduction of a troupe of captive-born western lowland gorillas in 2003 which The Aspinall Foundation spearheaded.

Damian Aspinall's soft spot for gorillas began when he was a child. One of his early memories is of a gorilla female who came and rescued him after he got stuck up a tree.

"She came up, put me on her back and climbed back down, wiped away my tears and spent the day comforting me."

John Aspinall and Zemo the tiger play together in the swimming pool. Zemo was the son of Tara, Aspinall's beloved first tigress, and was hand raised by Min Aspinall, John's second wife.

In his book, The Best of Friends, John recalls:

"All tigers are natural swimmers and I can personally confirm that they can easily outdistance a man in the water...Though a strong free-styler, Zemo could catch me with the greatest of ease."

Images of Zemo playing in the pool with John and Min can be seen in the 1983 video documentary by Roy Deverell, A Passion to Protect.

John Aspinall, with gorilla female, Juju and her baby, Kijo. Kijo, born on 2 April 1975, was special because he was the first gorilla to be bred by John Aspinall in captivity. His mother was born in the wild whilst his father, Kisoro, was a loan from Lincoln Park Zoo in Chicago. Through this success, John showed that, contrary to popular belief, gorillas could be successfully bred in captivity, provided they were given the right living conditions, including enough space, mental stimulation, social interaction with peers, and dietary variety to allow them to thrive.

John showing his playful side with one of the chimpanzees that used to be kept at Howletts. Unlike the gorilla, which is more reserved by nature, the chimp is quite extrovert. In John's words:

"The lesser ape wears his heart on his sleeve."

Damian with his youngest daughter, Freya, whose mother is television personality Donna Air. When she is with her father at Howletts, Freya loves to spend time with the many creatures her father knows so well. She is particularly fond of playing with the tiger cubs and does quite a mean tiger vocalisation.

One of John Aspinall's closest friends from his days at Oxford university, the businessman and MP, Sir James Goldsmith frequently advised John on business matters and was his biggest financial backer. It was Goldsmith that came to the rescue when the parks ran into money troubles after the stock market crash of 1973. Goldsmith also helped John to purchase Port Lympne and was instrumental in setting up The Aspinall Foundation as a registered charity. The Goldsmith family continue to maintain an interest in TAF: Goldsmith's daughter, Jemima Khan, was a guest of honour at Ambam, the gorilla's 24th birthday party. His sons, Zac and Ben Goldsmith are TAF Trustees, as is Robin Birley, Goldsmith's step son.

In the Aspinall household, everyone took their turn to pitch in. Here, Beryl Addley, the family nanny, draws the winning numbers for a 'Save the Gorilla' raffle. Over the years, Beryl's charges have consisted of both humans and animals. In fact, she probably brought up more baby animals at Howletts than human children! These have included Nuschka the wolf and a gorilla called Djoum, who grew up to become one of the largest silverbacks in the UK. Nanny Addley used to push him around in Damian and Amanda's old pram when he was a youngster.

James Osborne, John's half-brother and Damian's uncle, with a female lynx named Suchana. Although retired now, he still takes a keen interest in TAF's conservation work and sometimes visits the parks to see some of his old friends.

Amos Courage is the son of Lady Sarah Aspinall from her first marriage to Piers Courage. After his father's tragic death in a motor racing accident, his mother remarried and Amos went to live at Howletts. As a child, he got to travel all over the world and witness his stepfather's conservation efforts firsthand. It was John Aspinall who inspired him to get involved with the conservation work of the charity when he got older.

(Left) John and Damian in Congo-Brazzaville, where John had a gorilla sanctuary built in 1987 to provide long term care and rehabilitation for orphaned and confiscated gorillas on behalf of the Congolese government. This went on to become TAF's flagship project. The first set of orphans, along with a bonobo (pygmy chimpanzee), arrived in 1989. TAF continues to run and maintain this programme as part of the "Projet Protection des Gorilles" (PPG), now located in two protected areas within the Batéké Plateau, one in Congo and one in Gabon.

John Aspinall with Jara, who he helped bring up with wife, Sally. John was fascinated with tigers from boyhood. He recalls that as a child,

"I liked cats and dogs, but they did not stir my imagination… I needed the tinge of unpredictability, of independence, to invite my full respect."

Fearless, he would constantly push the boundaries of what was commonly considered safe when it came to interacting with so-called dangerous predators such as tigers. After a visit to Howletts, J. Paul Getty, the US businessman wrote to John, remarking that,

"Your friendship with tigers and wolves was something I always thought impossible. Your tigers and wolves seem to be as fond of you and as harmless as my Alsatians are to me."

Damian Aspinall with Dudhwa the Bengal tiger. John taught Damian that fear and respect go hand in hand, and that it is these two qualities that allow humans to develop close bonds with wild animals.

The suede jacket that you see John wearing in the previous picture was a favourite of the tigers, who loved to lick it. After John's death, Damian kept the jacket and still puts it on if he is going in with the tigers, who perhaps can smell their old friend, John after all these years.

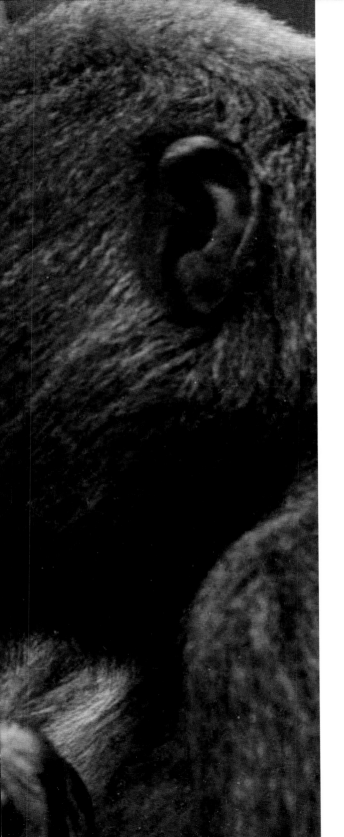

The Aspinall children were, in the words of their father,

"reared in a nursery full of gorilla babies and tiger cubs"

Here, a very young Damian Aspinall and his sister, Amanda, revel in some precious playtime with some of the animals in the gardens of Howletts where they grew up. Like her grandmother and step-mother before her, Amanda would go on to hand-rear a number of orphaned animals, including a wild boar 'squeaker' called Yiddle, as well as a number of timber wolves and tiger cubs. As John's eldest son, Damian was John's natural successor and takes his role as Chairman of TAF very seriously.

(Left) Keeping alive the family tradition - Damian's first daughter, Tansy, as a baby with Sangha being supervised by granddad. John would regularly take his own children, including Damian, into the primate enclosures as toddlers. According to John, his youngest child, Bassa, was

"shoved in with adult gorillas when he was only six months old"

– a custom kept up by Damian, who introduced Tansy and Clary to their first gorilla at a similar age.

"I used to love entering the gorillas' enclosure and going down the slide. It was like a huge playground for us." TANSY ASPINALL

Tansy (older child) and Clary (toddler) Aspinall, Damian's first two daughters, are pictured here playing with some of the female gorillas in the enclosure at Howletts. Now both young adults, the girls still make a point of going to see their childhood friends whenever they come home for family visits.

"If one had to pick an animal as a foster-mother to a human baby, I would unhesitatingly choose the terrestrial gorilla." JOHN ASPINALL

Damian's middle daughter, Clary, being introduced to Sounda, a female gorilla, as her father had been as a baby.

Sounda the Gorilla

One of the three so-called 'Brazzaville Orphans,' Sounda was initially taken in by Yvette Leroy, the French expatriate responsible for saving Djala . In an old TAF newsletter, John Aspinall relates that:

"In the Congo, Yvette's remarkable achievement with Djala became well-known, and some of the gorilla babies that, in the natural course of events, would have been smuggled to the Eastern Block, found their way to her. In a few years, she had seven orphans in her home..."

Three were given to the President of Senegal as a gift of state. On Yvette's suggestion, the remaining four were donated to Howletts to 'follow in the footsteps of Djala.' However, when John applied to the DoE for an import permit, he was turned down. A public campaign ensued, which led to a reversal of this decision. Unfortunately, in the interim, one of the babies died. John finishes the story:

"The remaining three, Kouillou (male), Sounda (female) and Sangha (female), arrived safely at Howletts accompanied by Yvette on the 19th of June 1987."

At the tender age of 10, Freya Aspinall is as comfortable around the animals in her father's wildlife parks as her siblings. Here she is pictured with a red-bellied lemur, a species that the charity is attempting to protect from extinction due to the ongoing threat of deforestation that it faces in its native Madagascar.

Damian Aspinall with his three daughters, Tansy (right), Clary (left) and Freya (centre) in the gorilla enclosure at Howletts Wild Animal Park. Although regulations prevented him from taking youngest daughter, Freya, into the gorilla enclosure as a baby, Damian Aspinall has gone to great lengths to ensure that all three of his children were given plenty of opportunity to develop close ties with these gentle creatures, just as he was as a boy.

Along the way, he has also taught them a few animal calls. According to eldest daughter, Tansy (right), the three sisters can do some pretty good animal vocalisations between them:

"My gorilla gurgle is quite good, my tiger is bad. Freya's is good. Dad plays 'guess the sound' with her. Clary's got a good gorilla gurgle too."

"In those days, the baby gorillas lived with my father and mother, and travelled wherever they went." DAMIAN ASPINALL

Damian's mother, Jane Gordon Hastings, pictured here in the 1950s with Baby Doll, one of the Aspinall family's first gorillas, in the car leaving London for Howletts.

Both Jane and her mother, Dorothy, helped to hand rear some of the first gorilla babies ever to arrive at Howletts.

Visitors to the village shop in Littlebourne were often greeted with the familiar sight of Damian's maternal grandmother, Dorothy Hastings, picking up a few bits, accompanied by one of the young gorillas from Howletts.

Here she is pictured with Shamba who arrived with Gugis at Howletts in the late 1950s aged two.

According to John's biographer, Brian Masters, many of the first baby gorillas were cared for "with exquisite love" by Mrs Hastings, who let them regularly sleep in her bed and "poured pure affection" on them.

Damian Aspinall with first wife Louise in the gorilla enclosure with
Sounda. The couple allowed their children to play with gorillas
from a very early age. Reflecting on what some considered to be a
controversial decision, Louise says,

*"For Damian and me, it was an honour to share our children
with a gorilla... it was incredibly emotional and a privilege."*

Over the years, Howletts and Port Lympne have been extremely successful at breeding animals in captivity.

Their breeding record, which to date includes some 136 gorillas, 35 eastern black rhinos, 139 clouded leopards, 42 Javan gibbons, 178 Javan langurs, 30 dusky leaf monkeys and 22 African elephants, shows what world leaders TAF has become in this arena.

Much of this has been attributed to the fact that the welfare and happiness of the animals in TAF's care is the charity's number one concern.

Donna Air, the mother of Freya Aspinall, has always been a big supporter of The Aspinall Foundation's work.

John with Omar (left) and Octavia (right), two of his Brazilian tapirs, giving him a good sniff. The nose clearly knows, as far as tapirs are concerned! Normally quite shy, these living fossils have bred well at Howletts - there are currently six in residence.

At Port Lympne, a colony of endangered Malayan tapirs have also successfully been reproducing and will hopefully be sent back to the wild soon. The latest arrival, a male infant named Kejutan, was born in 2011 and became the ninth tapir to be born at the park.

(Left) John Aspinall with Shamba (mother) and baby Mamba at Howletts. Shamba was one of the very first gorillas that John acquired. She arrived in July 1958 as a two year-old.

According to John,

"I first met the great ape in R.M. Ballantyne's absurd book The Gorilla Hunters at the age of about twelve, and later I saw him on screen in King Kong....Even in these dim works the mystic allure of the gorilla came through for me in unmistakable terms - it became my ambition to have gorillas as my friends, to win their confidence and trust."

John Aspinall with two of the species that he managed to successfully breed at Howletts and Port Lympne – elephants and gorillas. John strongly believed that wildlife parks should not serve simply to satisfy the curiosity of the public but should be primarily used as breeding sanctuaries where the world's most endangered wildlife species could be rescued from extinction, safely bred and then, wherever possible, returned back to their natural habitats. This view is shared by his son, Damian and is one of the main driving forces behind TAF's 'Back to the Wild' programme.

Lady Sarah Aspinall, John's third wife, with Canadian timber wolves, Bundle and Taihi.

favourite animals

Tara the Tiger

Tara, John Aspinall's first tigress, who was purchased from Harrods as a cub of nine weeks, was one of the loves of John's life and in his words, ' a mind-opener'. Prompted by a desire to create a proper home for her after she outgrew his flat in Belgravia, John bought Howletts, which is how the park first got started. An especially sweet natured, affectionate creature, John was heartbroken when she was killed by her mate in a freak accident in 1970. She is buried next to John and Min's daughter Mameena, who died in infancy, and another favourite gorilla, Djoum, at Howletts. Her genes survive in the many descendants she gave birth to during her adult lifetime which still populate the two parks.

Belinda 'Min' Aspinall, John's second wife, seen here nursing some tiger cubs, a task she found great solace in after losing her own child in infancy.

Amos Courage, Damian's step brother, is TAF's Director of Overseas Projects. For many years, Amos lived in Africa where he worked, first with a well-known documentary filmmaker in Zaire and later, in the Congo, where he helped to run the charity's gorilla rehabilitation centres, often putting himself in great personal danger due to the political instability in the region and the hazards that come from working out in the bush. After John's death in 2000, he returned to the UK to live at Howletts. He now divides his time between Kent and Africa, managing TAF's conservation efforts abroad.

Damian Aspinall as a young boy at Howletts, playing with one of the tiger cubs. He has always maintained that he had a very remarkable childhood as far as early experiences with animals are concerned, and feels it gave him some rare insights into the animal mind, which helps to guide him in making decisions about the direction of TAF's work today.

In the early years, the animals used to roam freely on the grounds at Howletts. In this picture, we see a typical Aspinall family scene from those days – John Aspinall, catching up with an old friend, Philip Martin in the parkland; and Damian as a boy, playing nearby with a gorilla.

The first African elephant ever to be born in captivity in the UK was at Howletts.

Sabi, a female calf, who was born on 25 May 1982 to mum, Masa, was the result of a 10 year breeding programme started by John Aspinall in the 1970s.

To date, Howletts has the largest African elephant herd in the UK and has had more births than all other British collections put together – **between 1994 and 2014, 14 out of 25 UK elephant births took place at Howletts and Port Lympne.**

John Aspinall with Torgamba, the Sumatran rhinoceros who came to Kent as part of the ground-breaking Sumatran Rhino Conservation Project initiated in 1984 in co-operation with the Indonesian government. The idea was to start a breeding colony of these extremely rare animals in Kent for reintroduction purposes. Torgamba arrived in 1986 to jubilant celebrations, and was named after the area where he was found. Renowned for his unusual russet colouring and friendly nature, he lived at Port Lympne until 1998, while a suitable partner was sought for him. Unfortunately, one was never found, so he was returned to the Sumatran Rhino Sanctuary in Way Kambas National Park where attempts to mate him with a female called Bina are ongoing.

At Howletts and Port Lympne, food is dropped from the top of primate enclosures, as if from trees, the idea being that it mimics the way that animals would forage in the wild. This method of feeding was pioneered by John Aspinall as early as the 1970s. In a booklet on Howletts published around 1975, he describes the daily feeding regime for the primates:

"Each morning, whatever the weather, we scatter nuts or raisins in this deep litter, which enables the apes to forage for an hour or two, after the manner of wild-living gorillas. At sundown we distribute fresh bales of clean straw to enable them to make their night nests."

Djoum the gorilla (above) holds a special place in the memories of the Aspinall family. Described by John as "self-confident", "good-natured" and full of life, he arrived at Howletts as a frightened and malnourished orphan badly in need of attention. Thanks to the care he received here, Djoum managed to overcome his traumatic background, growing into one of the largest captive silverbacks in the UK. Despite his enormous size, he still allowed people into his enclosure, even as a full-grown adult.

John was fond of saying that Djoum was one of the biggest successes of his life and his greatest wild animal friend. Sadly, on 19 April 1997, Djoum died of heart failure, aged 29. He was buried in the family cemetery at Howletts, and a bronze statue was erected in the mansion gardens in his memory.

(Right) Ambam, the lowland gorilla male famous for walking upright, celebrated his 24th birthday in April 2014, very close to the date of TAF's 30th anniversary.

Howletts and Port Lympne have the largest collection of critically endangered western lowland gorillas in the world. Since the birth of Kijo at Port Lympne Reserve in April 1975, a total of **136 gorillas** have been born as part of TAF-led breeding programmes. **These have produced 70% of all UK captive births for this species in the last 20 years.**

As passionate about conservation as Damian Aspinall, HRH Prince William, who is patron of wildlife charity, the Tusk Trust, popped down to Port Lympne Reserve in the summer of 2012. Here he was given a tour by Damian and his youngest daughter, Freya, which included hand feeding some of the animals. The main reason for his visit, though, was to give a royal send off to three black rhino: two females named Grumeti and Zawadi and one male named Monduli, who were being prepared for reintroduction into the African wilderness as part of TAF's 'Back to the Wild' programme. Black rhino are considered to be the most critically endangered of all the three remaining rhino subspecies in Africa, where they have been poached virtually into extinction for their horns. Footage of the occasion was featured in the BBC documentary, The Prince, The Poacher And The Rhino.

"To him, all creatures were reflections of a universal spirit which each expressed in his or her individual and unique way. It was that divine spark which he cherished in his animals. They seemed, to John, to fulfil the qualities that made life worth living: always true to themselves; never pretentious; seeking at all times to fulfil their potential." HENRY KISSINGER

Former US Secretary of State, Henry Kissinger (front) with John Aspinall and the South African conservationist, Dr Ian Player (rear left), brother of golfing legend Gary Player, on a visit to Howletts.

Margaret Thatcher on a private visit to Howletts. The former Prime Minister had been a contemporary of John's at Oxford, and in 1985, she had helped him to broker an agreement with the Indonesian government to help save the Sumatran rhino, which was close to extinction. As a result, Port Lympne managed to secure Torgamba, a male Sumatran rhino, who lived at Port Lympne for thirteen years before being returned by TAF to a captive breeding centre in Sumatra in 1998.

The Sumatran rhino is the smallest member of the rhinoceros family and is distinguished by skin with an unusually attractive reddish hue, covered with hair. It's closest genetic ancestor is the well-known woolly mammoth we know about from the fossil record.

Sadly, this species has been hunted virtually to extinction for its horn – in 1995, there were only 200-300 left in the whole world. It was the cause of the Sumatran rhino that served as the immediate catalyst for the establishment of The Aspinall Foundation in 1984 in the lead up to talks with the Indonesia government about starting a conservation and breeding programme.

The President of Gabon, Mr Ali Bongo Ondimba, on a visit to Port Lympne Reserve with Damian Aspinall. Having travelled to London for the 2012 Olympic Games, he was keen to make a detour to Kent to witness firsthand the TAF gorilla breeding programmes that Damian, as Chairman of The Aspinall Foundation, now heads up. All of the gorillas that are reintroduced to Africa from Howletts and Port Lympne are sent to the Batéke Plateau National Park in south-east Gabon. Close collaboration with the government has been essential to the success of the project and helps to ensure that the animals continue to be guarded against potential attacks from poachers.

Dheddi the Capuchin Monkey

favourite animals

A rescue from Harrods in the 1950s, Dheddi, which is short for 'Dead Loss', was John and Jane Aspinall's first exotic animal – in the West, capuchin monkeys were once quite commonly sold as pets. The monkey was in such poor shape that John didn't think he would last more than a few days, hence his name. John explains:

"He was in a sorry state when I saw him…covered in sores and bald patches…and I bought him out of pity for his condition and admiration for the spirit that illumined his frightened but courageous little eyes."

Instead of dying, he lived to become the founding father of Port Lympne's capuchin colony and enjoyed a very long life – passing away in 1991. His many descendants make him one of the reserve's true founders!

"I'm happiest with the animals... I find peace among them. When I'm with them, the world stops and nothing else matters."

DAMIAN ASPINALL

Having been around animals all his life, Damian Aspinall has a deep and instinctive knowledge of the psychology and behaviour of many wild animals that is the envy of any biologist. As well as being able to understand the calls and grunts of gorillas, he can also mimic and interpret those of tigers, rhino, wolves, monkeys and red river hogs.

His unique childhood relationships with animals mean that he is ideally placed to understand their needs and to advocate for them, especially as they have no voice of their own.

Howletts

Currently the Aspinall family home, Howletts was originally built in 1787–9 for Isaac Baugh, a merchant of the East India Company. Designed by Sir John Leach (1760-1834), its Roman-style pediment facade and columned portico make it a prime example of the Neo-Palladian revival so popular with the Georgians. However, by the time John Aspinall acquired Howletts in 1957, which he paid for with a big win at the horses, much of its clean lines and symmetrical proportions were obscured from view by years of alterations, additions and neglect. At great expense, Aspinall had the house restored with the help of architect Phillip Jebb; and interior designer, John Fowler, with Russell Page employed to advise on the woodland and gardens.

The name 'Howletts' appears to be very ancient, deriving from the medieval, 'Owlet', and records show that the estate itself dates back to at least the fifteenth century when it was owned by the Isaac family of Patrixbourne. The manor remained in their hands until Tudor times after which it came into the possession of Sir Henry Palmer, an admiral in Henry the VIII's navy. Rather fittingly, Howletts was later bought by the famous Regency gambler, Sir Thomas Gering, who lost the whole estate in a game of faro one evening at White's Club in London before falling into disrepair under the ownership of an aged Australian magnate called Ramsey who acquired it after the war and lived in what was by then a crumbling ruin until his death at the age of 97.

The mansion currently sits in close to 100 acres of beautiful parkland, much of it now devoted to the wild animal park. It is thought that some of the trees found here may be at least 500 years old. Several specimens, including a fruiting gingko biloba, turkey oak, several ilexes, Lebanon cedars, cypresses and an exceedingly majestic sequoia, probably formed part of the arboretum planted by Abraham Gipps, a later owner of the property, whose ancestors founded Martin's Bank. In recent years, some of these have been declared protected specimens, such as the famous Howletts Chestnut, thought to be one of the largest of its kind in England.

John Aspinall bought Howletts in 1957 following a considerable win on a horse called Prelone in the Cesarewitch Handicap at Newmarket. Interestingly, just a few centuries before, one of its previous owners, Thomas Dering, lost the whole estate one evening in a gamble.

Also located in the grounds of Howletts are two gorilla statues: The first is a bronze statue of Djoum, the first adult male silverback to allow the Aspinall family to enter his enclosure, who is depicted along with one of his children; another is of Gugis, from whom John Aspinall learnt a great deal about gorilla behaviour.

The parkland at Howletts is very old, with many trees, such as the famous Howletts Chestnut, dating back to at least the 15th century. John recounts in his book:

"The gardens were redesigned by Russell Page around the remarkable Spanish chestnuts, cedars of Lebanon and ilex trees which have been a feature of the park for centuries."

'Howletts' is an ancient name, thought to have evolved from the Tudor word 'Owlet', though no one is quite sure whether this has any connection to baby birds or not. Legend has it that bad luck will befall anyone who tries to change the title of the estate. Certainly, that is what John Aspinall was told by a wisened local villager after she overheard him proclaiming his desire to rename the place. Being the sort of man he was, he decided it was better not to tempt fate!

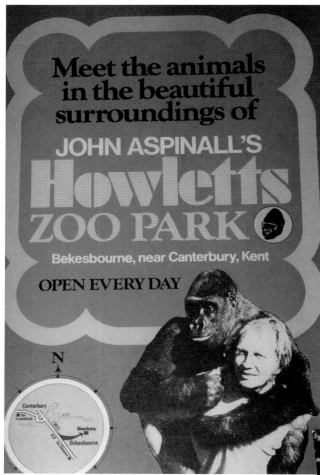

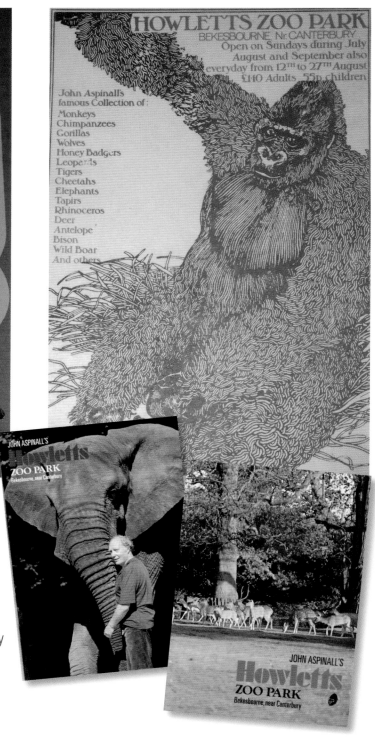

A selection of marketing posters and brochures used to promote Howletts over the years. Originally a private zoo, John decided that he needed the financial support of the public if he was to transform his personal hobby into a more serious conservation effort. As a result, 'Howletts Zoo Park' opened to the public in 1975.

Howletts is the only animal collection to house grizzled leaf monkeys outside of their native country and is a world leader in breeding the endangered Javan gibbon. **Since 1994, 29 of the 31 gibbon births in the UK have been at a TAF-run park.**

John Aspinall's biographer, Brian Masters, pointed out that John got very little credit for his loving and authentic restoration of not just Howletts, but also the mansion at Port Lympne and several period properties in London. In all cases, no expense was spared, with the renovation of the mansion taking nearly five years. Today, Howletts is a listed building. This view, of the north-west front of the house, shows its handsome symmetrical proportions, which are perfectly offset by the Roman-style urns and stone balustrade, fittingly flanked by a pair of lions.

At Howletts, the gardens and parkland are not only decorative, but are also used by the horticultural team at the wildlife park to grow a range of herbs and browsing material for the animals.

Every day, new leaves are collected from the woods on the estate, along with edible plants such as sunflowers, lavender and banana leaves, which are cultivated in the walled garden. These are fed to the animals to ensure they get a balanced and varied diet.

(Opposite page) John Aspinall died in 2000 of cancer. His body was buried in the grounds of Howletts, directly in front of the house he so lovingly restored. A memorial globe etched with the names of friends and loved ones, was erected to mark his grave.

Port Lympne

The elegant Edwardian mansion that stands at the centre of the vast Port Lympne estate was the creation of the renowned English architect, Sir Herbert Baker (1862-1946). Famous for designing a host of government buildings and stately residences, both in the UK and the British colonies, Baker was a native of Kent whose family home was, rather appropriately, considering the Aspinall link, named 'Owletts'.

Designed to capture the classical spirit of the estate's ancient past, the house was built in 1912 for Sir Phillip Sassoon, the baronet, MP and former private secretary to David Lloyd George. Situated on the sunny southern slopes of the Kentish downs, overlooking the English Channel, the mansion was constructed using the finest materials available, including handmade French red bricks, English oak window frames, Kentish roof tiles and stained Oregon pine wood rafters.

Phillip Tilden (1887-1956) was commissioned to create the eclectic but opulent interiors, from the Moorish-style courtyard to the Neo-classical octagonal library, built especially for peace talks leading up to the Treaty of Paris, which was signed here in the summer of 1921.

The 1923 issue of Country Life magazine described it as *'the most remarkable modern house in England,'* and of such exceptional *'beauty, proportion and balance'* that it was sure to evoke a sense of wonder in even the most world weary visitor. Certainly, Port Lympne impressed John Aspinall enough

to buy it in the winter of 1973. Despite its derelict condition after two world wars, John recognised the enormous potential the then 300-acre estate offered to his family and ever-expanding wildlife collection as a consequence of its sheltered, south-facing position and generous expanse of parkland.

The terraced gardens were restored to their former glory with the help of Russell Page and a team of gardeners. Today Port Lympne is renowned for its herbaceous borders, chequerboard and striped gardens, and commanding York stone stairway, a heady combination that has made it a favourite with wedding parties and celebrity gardeners alike.

From its very beginnings, Port Lympne was designed to host visitors and parties. Over the years, an array of illustrious and notable guests have crossed its threshold, from nobility (Lord Curzon, Lord Mountbatten) to royalty (Prince Edward VIII and Wallace Simpson); celebrities like Charlie Chaplin and TE Lawrence (better known as Lawrence of Arabia) and statesmen (Lloyd George, Wegend, Foch, Millerand, Clemenceau, Briand).

In keeping with this tradition of hospitality, the Port Lympne mansion was recently converted into a boutique hotel, complete with six luxurious themed bedrooms and suites, and opened to the public in the summer of 2014.

Conscious of the space limitations at Howletts and keen to find a suitable stretch of Kentish parkland nearby, John Aspinall bought the Port Lympne estate near Folkestone in 1973.

Many people do not know that Port Lympne was actually John's second attempt at expansion. His first, at Chilham Park near Canterbury, failed because he couldn't get the necessary planning permission from the local council. Five years later, however, things had changed:

"By now the relevant authorities had decided that I was no safari-park entrepreneur or circus impresario. Permission was granted and Port Lympne Wildlife Sanctuary and Gardens opened to the public in the early summer of 1976."

Designed by Herbert Baker, the English architect famous for his many state buildings and monuments in South Africa and India, the mansion at Port Lympne shows the clear influence of his colonial experience. This can be seen in the Cape Dutch-style twin gables and colonnades on the south front, which bear a striking resemblance to Groote Schuur, the residence in Cape Town that Baker designed for Cecil John Rhodes.

According to an old Port Lympne brochure,

"Baker took full advantage of the magnificent site and an almost unlimited budget to produce what is generally regarded as his masterpiece."

During the 1920s and 30s, the house welcomed many notable politicians of the day, including Winston Churchill, David Lloyd George, and the French prime ministers, Georges Clemenceau and Aristide Briand.

The octagonal library was created as a miniaturised version of the Radcliff Camera, designed by James Gibbs in the Neo-Palladian style to house the science collection which still forms part of the Bodleian Library at Oxford University. Both Phillip Sassoon and John Aspinall were educated there, though of course, John never graduated, famously choosing to go to the races instead of sit for his final exams.

The walls and book cases are made from panels of unstained sycamore wood, which according to an old Port Lympne guide book, were *'supposedly at the request of Clemenceau himself.'*

Sir Phillip, who was an MP for Hythe and private secretary to both Lord Haig and later, David Lloyd George, let Port Lympne be used for several peace conferences.

During the 1921 peace talks that led up the singing of the Treaty of Paris, a hot line to the Elysée Palace was installed in the octagonal library, which was especially built for the occasion, so that the visiting French prime minister had access to his advisers during his five-week stay here.

A 1923 article in Country Life sums it up nicely, when it remarks:

"Whatever the nature of the councils, they had a superb setting, combining the dignity suitable for such encounters with the intimacy that was their essence."

TAF's wildlife parks have the **largest captive breeding herd of Eastern black rhinoceros outside of Africa.** Since 1994, **19 out of the 31 black rhino births in the UK** have been at a TAF-managed park.

One of the most distinctive features about Port Lympne has always been its situation, looking out from its elevated position on the edge of the North Downs towards the English Channel. Below, John Aspinall eloquently lists what he considered to be the property's main virtues:

"...nearly 300 acres of ornamental parkland, amphitheatrical in shape and facing south – protected on three sides by belts of broadleaf woodland – overlooking the Channel with a fair view to France...the whole crowned by a fine red-brick mansion, itself garlanded by 15 acres of terraced gardens."

According to John Aspinall,

"Sassoon was captivated by the associations the area had with the Romans...and the garden has a distinctly Roman or Italian feeling."

This helps to explain the classical plinths and Romanesque porticos that used to form part of the dramatic Trojan Stairway.

Built entirely from York stone, it has undergone a gradual transformation since Sassoon's time, the more obviously Roman features giving way to a more modern, paired-down look, softened by pots of greenery. (right) The formality of the clipped evergreen hedges remain, although the original cypress hedging was replaced by John for more frost-resistant leylandii.

Country Life magazine waxed lyrical about the stairway, proclaiming:

"A mystic importance attaches to steps. They symbolise civilisation, human life, the upward struggle of existence."

If you have ever tried to climb all 125 steps in one go, you'll know that this is certainly true, if only from a physical perspective! Still, the panoramic views from the top certainly make it worth the effort...

The name, 'Port Lympne' derives from an ancient Roman settlement nearby called Portus Lemanis (which translates to 'the port of Lympne'). It was once thought to have been a safe stopping off point for sea traders making the perilous journey along Britain's south coast from Dover to the Isle of Wight via Chichester.

When John Aspinall bought Port Lympne, it had not been lived in since the war. As a result, the grounds had to be re-established with the help of a team of gardeners. Guidance was sought from the well-known garden designer and landscaper, Russell Page, who had written about it in an article for 'The Listener' in 1934.

Recalling what took place in an early brochure, John explains:

"Russell Page wrote over 40 years ago that no gardens in England have a more beautiful setting than Port Lympne. When I asked him for advice on these gardens that he knew so well before the war, I ventured the opinion that in spite of all the effort we intended to make, they would never be as beautiful as they were in his youth. He surprised me by countering that they should be even more lovely and spectacular…The garden, he emphasised, had gained by the growth and mellowing of the surrounding trees."

Luckily, the site at Port Lympne benefits from a sloping, south-facing position, making it easy to grow and lay out an endless array of garden 'rooms' along its many terraces, which today include the striped and chessboard gardens.

Dotted around the terraces are a number of statues and ornaments, including several stone herms (ancient fertility symbols) sculpted by Jean Michiel Rysbrack (1694-1770), bought by Sassoon from Stowe House in Buckinghamshire, as well as two bronze hippos by the South African sculptor, Donald Grieg, which form part of the pond on the upper terrace.

The majestic herbaceous borders, which measure some 135 feet in length, continue to provide plenty of seasonal interest throughout the year and are often used as a backdrop for wedding photographs.

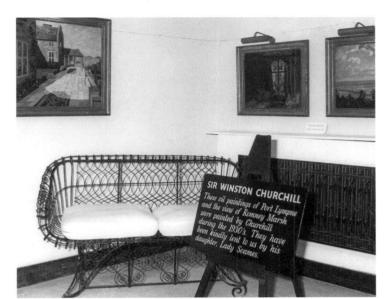

A Sotheby's catalogue relates that,

"Churchill was a frequent visitor to Sir Philip Sassoon's house at Lympne, using these holidays as necessary respites from the stress of political life, but also as an opportunity to focus on writing his war memoirs and to paint. For him painting provided a relief: he needed to engage alternative parts of his mind through pursuits which required focus and concentration in order to silence the thoughts which occupied the majority of his days."

During one of his stays, he painted this view of the south side of the mansion – a little known fact discovered by John Aspinall after he bought the estate. As part of his restoration plans, John approached Churchill's daughter, Lady Mary Soames, about displaying the painting at Port Lympne. Luckily for Aspinall, she was happy to oblige. For many years, it hung on the walls of the house as a loan from the Churchill family, but recently it was returned to Chartwell where it can be seen as part of the National Trust Collection.

As impressive as any of the rooms is the entrance hall, with its marble columns and intricate floor mosaic, made of concentric rings of black and white marble tiles. Each tile was individually crafted by hand and is completely unique, making it, in the words of a previous brochure,

"an extraordinary tour de force, well beyond the capacity of present day craftsmen."

Country Life magazine described it as:

"…a simple conception in black and white, with black and white marble paving arranged in fascinating gradations of the triangle, so that the sharper the perspective, the deeper the triangles appear. The execution of the work is admirable, seeing that the shapes of the pieces are constantly varying."

As part of his grand design scheme, Sir Phillip Sassoon decided to commission a number of famous artists, many of whom were fairly unknown at the time, to decorate the walls of his reception rooms with a series of unique paintings. These include Rex Whistler (1905-1944), who produced the famous tented room you can see further on; and Jose Maria Sert (1874-1945), the Spanish painter who decorated the drawing room (above) with a bright mural filled with images of elephants, tropical birds and lush vegetation. Sadly, it was destroyed by troops posted here during the Second World War, but luckily for us, was preserved for posterity through photographs such as this one, which was originally published in the May 1923 issue of Country Life magazine.

One of the real treasures of the Port Lympne interior is the tented Rex Whistler Room. Created by the Kent-born painter and designer for Sir Phillip Sassoon in the 1930s, when he was still relatively unknown, the trompe l'oeil Georgian style murals and cartouche of the original garden plan that decorate the walls are considered to be some of the British artist's finest surviving works.

After the Second World War, which sadly took Whistler's life, the murals were restored by experts from the Tate Britain, a task that took nearly a year to complete. They remain an integral part of the mansion's history and design to this day.

To replace the Sert mural that was destroyed during the war, John Aspinall commissioned the wildlife artist, Spencer Roberts to paint a mural in the former drawing room of the mansion in 1985.

The result was a compelling mixture of fantasy and reality that cleverly incorporates many features of the room. One of Roberts' largest paintings, the mural was themed around the flora and fauna of south east Asia, and depicts over 200 different species of animal and bird including Sumatran rhinoceros, Asian lion and elephant and snow leopards.

As part of plans to help fund the charity's conservation work and give visitors the opportunity to enjoy a truly unforgettable wildlife experience, Port Lympne began to add overnight accommodation facilities to the grounds a few years ago, including Livingstone and Elephant Lodges, two luxury 'glamping' experiences set in the extensive grounds of the reserve, offering great views of the animal enclosures.

In keeping with this tradition of hospitality, the Port Lympne mansion was recently converted into a boutique hotel, complete with six luxurious themed bedrooms and suites, and opened to the public on 13 June 2014.

The opening was inaugurated by the MP for Hythe, Damian Collins – a fitting nod to the past, given that its original owner, Sir Phillip Sassoon also once held that office.

To reflect the recent changes, the estate was also renamed 'Port Lympne Reserve.'

"Many years ago, it became clear to me that Howletts with its mere sixty acres could not contain for long the burgeoning colonies of wild animals that were breeding there so profusely…After a seven year quest, we stumbled on Port Lympne and it would be hard to imagine a more suitable property for the purposes we had in mind."

JOHN ASPINALL

a unique ethos

Animal wellbeing and wildlife conservation lies at the heart of everything that The Aspinall Foundation does. This ethos of putting animals first extends to the way TAF runs its two Kent wildlife parks, which are considered, first and foremost, to be sanctuaries for the conservation, breeding and reintroduction of rare and endangered animals.

This means trying, wherever possible, to replicate the conditions these creatures would enjoy in their natural habitats, even if it doesn't make commercial sense, and treating them with the dignity and respect that they deserve. As a result, many of the enclosures are designed to make their inhabitants feel safe, stimulated and at home enough to breed without disruption, rather than to make them easy for visitors to spot. It is also why Howletts and Port Lympne go to great lengths to provide a wide variety of fresh browse and food for their animal guests, so that they get the full range of nutrients and daily stimulation they need to thrive.

The strategy seems to have paid off : over the years, both centres have gained an outstanding reputation for breeding successes, often with animals previously thought impossible to rear in captivity. Since the birth of Howlett's first litter of clouded leopards in 1970, widely regarded as one of the most difficult cat species to breed, TAF has gone on to produce the world's first captive-born honey badgers (1972); the UK's first white fronted capuchin monkey (1972), as well as the first British-born African elephant (1982), Javan gibbon (1988) and brown hyena (2009).

TAF has also successfully managed to breed Przewalski horses, once thought to be extinct in the wild; and also Barbary lions that are now completely extinct in the wild. To date, Howletts is also the only institution outside of Indonesia to keep and breed Heck's macaques. You can catch a glimpse of some these rare and beautiful creatures, along with their offspring, in the pages that follow.

comparative list of breeding successes

SPECIES	TOTAL BIRTHS 1950–2014	COMPARATIVE CAPTIVE BIRTHS 1994–2014		PERCENTAGE
	PL & H	PL & H	UK	
Eastern black rhino	35	19	31	61%
African elephant	22	14	25	56%
Javan gibbon	42	29	31	90%
Clouded leopard	139	47	58	81%
Javan langur	178	130	181	75%
Dusky leaf monkey	30	26	57	46%
Western lowland gorilla	136	81	118	69%

first births celebrated by TAF

1970   The first UK-bred clouded leopard, widely regarded as one of the most difficult cat species to breed in captivity, is born at Howletts.

May 1971   The first Przewalksi horse foal is born at Howletts. At this stage, it was considered to be extinct in the wild.

1972   The first captive-born honey badger in the world is born at Howletts.

1972   The first white fronted capuchin monkey ever to be born in the UK is bred at Howletts.

1974   The first roan antelope is born at Howletts.

April 1975   Kijo, a male gorilla, is the first of his species to be born at an Aspinall-owned wildlife park. Today, both Kent parks have the largest collection of western lowland gorillas in the world.

1977   First births of banded langur, white-faced Saki monkeys.

1977   Basha, the first black rhino is born to mother, Naivasha. Together, the two Kent parks boast the largest captive breeding herd of Eastern black rhinoceros outside of Africa.

1980   The first Barbary lion cub is born. Howletts and Port Lympne were the first UK parks to keep Barbary lions, now extinct in the wild.

May 1982   Birth of Sabi, the first African elephant to be born in captivity in the UK. The African elephant herd at Howletts is the largest in the UK and has had more births than all other British collections combined.

1983   The first Indian desert cat cub is born.

1984   The first Javan langur is born. To date, both TAF-managed parks boast a record of 178 births of this endangered species.

1986   The first fishing cat cub is born. TAF is considered to be one of the most successful breeders of this species in the world.

1986   The first rusty-spotted cat cub is born at Port Lympne – a UK first for this species!

1988   Howletts celebrates the birth of the first red-shanked Douc langur – another UK first.

1988   Howletts produces the first Javan gibbon baby in the UK. To date, both TAF-managed parks have seen 42 births of this rare animal.

1991   The first banded langur is born.

1999   The first grizzled langur to be born in captivity in the UK, is born at Howletts.

2006   Another UK first: Port Lympne celebrates the first greater bamboo lemur birth.

2009   The first brown hyena to be born in the UK is reared at a TAF-run park in Kent.

Nov 2009   The first Heck's macaque baby is born. Howletts is currently the only wild animal park outside of Indonesia to house and breed with this species.

Fishing cat

Clouded leopard

TAF is the largest breeder of clouded leopards in the UK, producing 47 of the 58 babies born between 1994-2014. For this reason, we have taken over the studbooks for this species of cat.

(Previous page) Siberian tigers

Serval cat

(Right) Panther

Barbary lions

Fossa

Barbary lions, which used to roam the Atlas Mountains in Morocco, are now extinct in the wild, the last time any were spotted was in the 1940s and 1950s. However, thanks to an international breeding programme, several lions carrying the barbary gene have been successfully bred at Port Lympne. In fact, the park is currently home to 10% of the world's existing population of this rare cat species, which TAF hopes to return to the wild one day in the future.

TAF's two wildlife sanctuaries are one of the **world's most successful breeders of fishing cats,** with the first cub being born in 1986.

(Left) Barbary lion cub

Fishing cat kittens

Four young cheetah cubs – right, an adult cheetah

Caracal cat

Pallas cat kitten

Snow leopard cubs

Lynx

Asian elephants – Howletts and Port Lympne

Between 1994 and 2014, 25 African elephants were born in captivity within the UK. Of these, 14 came from Howletts, including the **very first African elephant calf born in England.**

African elephants

(Left) Giraffes and wildebeest – African Experience, Port Lympne Reserve.

Bush dog

African painted dogs

Honey badger

Zebras

In the last twenty years, 19 out of the 31 black rhino births in the UK have been at a TAF-managed park. Port Lympne Reserve currently has **the largest captive breeding herd of this species outside of Africa.**

Black rhinos

Warty pigs

Blackbuck calf

Giant anteater

Blackbuck

(Overleaf) A family of dhole

Przewalksi horses

Over the years, The Aspinall Foundation's two parks have successfully housed and bred species such as the Atlas or Barbary lion and Przewalksi horse. The former species has been totally wiped out in the wild, while the latter was once considered to be completely extinct in the wild until quite recently.

In 1993, TAF sent 10 Przewalksi horses back to China where they have slowly begun to repopulate an area that was once their natural home. One mare was also sent to the Hustain Nuruu Steppe Reserve in Mongolia in 1996 as part of a collaborative reintroduction project established two years previously.

(Right) Red pandas

Dusky langur

Greater bamboo lemur

Black lemur

Gugis the Gorilla

Gugis the gorilla arrived at Howletts as a 10-month old in December 1958 and would grow into the park's first adult male silverback. He was the first male in the group and as such, became a test case, allowing John Aspinall to discover first hand the nature and behaviour of gorillas. Sadly, he proved to be infertile and a difficult study because, unlike many of the other gorillas, he was able to disguise his moods from humans. Even so, John learnt much from him during his 19 years of life, which he went on to share with the rest of the zoo-keeping fraternity. Sadly, on 24 March 1977, he died suddenly from unsuspected bronchial pneumonia. A statue dedicated to his memory was later erected and can still be seen in the grounds of Howletts Wild Animal Park.

Francois' Langur

Crowned sifaka lemur

Douc langur

Crowned lemur

Javan gibbon

Colobus monkey

TAF-led breeding programmes have accounted for over 90% of all Javan gibbons born in captivity in the UK in the last twenty years. It is a world leader in breeding this endangered primate and looks after the studbook for this species.

Guinea baboon

The primates at Howletts and Port Lympne are fed a variety of fresh organically grown herbs, which are cultivated especially for them. Unlike many other zoos, these animals are fed up to 120 different varieties of fresh fruit, vegetables, leaves and herbs every day, much of which is either sourced from trees in the parks' woodlands or grown on local farms nearby. Exotic fruits are sourced from markets in London.

Javan ebony langur

Three-quarters of all Javan langurs born in captivity in Britain are born at a TAF-run animal park. The charity also runs the only breeding programme for Heck's macaques outside of Indonesia, celebrating its first birth in 2009.

De Brazza's monkey baby

Saki monkey

Heck's macaque

(Overleaf) Gorillas

Put together, Howletts and Port Lympne have the **largest collection of critically endangered western lowland gorillas in the world**. Since 1950, they have managed to breed 136 gorillas, producing **81 out of the 118** UK captive gorilla births in the last twenty years.

Western lowland gorilla

Boredom and lack of social stimulus are the enemy to breeding when it comes to intelligent primates like gorillas. To keep the animals happy, they are kept in large family groups, given a wide variety of fresh herbs and fruit every day, and encouraged to forage amongst the straw bedding by dropping food from the top of enclosures – as if it had fallen from the trees. All of these techniques were first pioneered at Howletts and Port Lympne by John Aspinall and developed by his son, Damian. Today, some have now become standard practice within the industry.

(Left) A baby gorilla

(Overleaf) Black howler monkey

"Zoos should be about animals, not people."

DAMIAN ASPINALL

Picking up the conservation mantle from his father, current TAF Chairman, Damian Aspinall's main focus is on using the sanctuary of the charity's two wildlife parks to nurture and breed rare and endangered animal species, with the aim of restoring their numbers to healthier levels and then re- introducing them back into the wild.

At Howletts and Port Lympne, the emphasis is therefore, not on providing entertainment for humans, but rather on maintaining the welfare of the animals, who are considered honoured guests. As far as Damian is concerned, animals come first. Period.

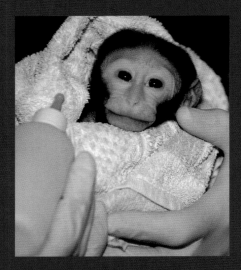

milestones:
the story so far

When John Aspinall formed the charity that bears his name in 1984, he saw it as a vehicle for fulfilling his ultimate ambition: to safeguard the survival of rare and endangered animal species, and conserve unspoiled wilderness for future generations. In his book, The Best of Friends (1976), he set out his credo:

"I believe that there is an outside chance to save the earth and most of its tenants. This outside chance must be grabbed with gambler's hands."

As early as the 1970s, Aspinall had the foresight to realise that man's avaricious habit of collecting exotic animals from around the world and keeping them in what were essentially little more than gilded cages, had severe limitations. As well as the negative impact it often had on the wellbeing of the animals themselves, it also helped fuel the cruel and destructive trade in exotic animals and animal products, which, at that stage, was only just beginning to be regulated.

Another, more sustainable way had to be found to conserve nature's precious creatures. But how might one tackle such an ambitious task? The answer, he decided, was to develop a network of wildlife sanctuaries for rescued and endangered species with specialised breeding programmes, which should, wherever possible, be attached to protected reserves where animals could ultimately be released and live as they were meant to: free, in healthy numbers and in ecosystems no longer under threat from humans.

John outlined his mission in the 1983 documentary, A Passion to Protect. The following year, he founded The Aspinall Foundation and threw himself into his first projects: a breeding and conservation programme for the Sumatran rhino; and the establishment of a primate rescue and rehabilitation centre in Africa, motivated by the obvious psychological distress he discerned in gorillas such as Djala and Kwibi, who arrived at Howletts traumatised from their

Since then, The Aspinall Foundation has grown from strength to strength. Under the leadership of John's son, Damian, the work of the charity is starting to come full circle, the numbers and types of species being reintroduced from its breeding programmes steadily increasing with each passing year.

What follows is a chronological account of TAF's remarkable journey and accomplishments since its inception nearly 30

In 1984, John Aspinall decided that the time had come to set up a charity to further his conservation aims, and so, on the 29th of April 1984, The Aspinall Foundation was born.

Alerted to the plight of the Sumatran rhino, already under threat from illegal logging and deforestation for agriculture, John embarked on a ground-breaking plan to establish a captive breeding and reintroduction programme for the species as a hedge against their increasingly likely extinction. Discussions got underway at a conference in Indonesia in 1984. This eventually led to the signing of an agreement between the charity and the Indonesian government, one that would become a cornerstone both for the future direction of the charity, and for worldwide efforts to save the species.

1985

On 24 May 1985, the Sumatran rhino conservation project was created. By August of 1985, a base-camp had been constructed in a forested area of Sumatra to study in more detail the largely unknown habits of this shy, nocturnal animal.

Later that same year, on the 25th of November 1985, the first Sumatran rhino was captured. Named Torgamba, after the region where he was found, he arrived at Howletts in 1986 to begin the captive breeding programme.

1986

Torgamba, the Sumatran rhino
arrived at Howletts.

That same year, a young gorilla named Djala was adopted from the Congo.
He, and the three gorilla orphans who followed him from Brazzaville, were to
prove the catalyst for what would go on to become TAF's flagship project: a
gorilla conservation programme in Africa.

1987

With importation laws becoming stricter in order to curb illegal wildlife trading, it became increasingly difficult for TAF to bring rescued animals to the UK for rehabilitation. In exchange for the adoption of three gorillas by the charity in 1987, TAF made an agreement with the Congolese government to develop an in-situ primate orphanage within a patch of woodland on the grounds of Brazzaville Zoo.

1989

Two years later, it became functional and received its first intake of orphaned gorillas, including Yambo (Sid), along with a bonobo (or pygmy chimpanzee) called Max.

1990

Considered to be the last truly wild horse, the Przewalski horse had
been categorised as 'extinct in the wild' during the 1960s. Dedicated
co-operative breeding programmes amongst institutions with
captive specimens meant that by the 1980s, some were able to be
reintroduced to their native Mongolia. After supporting these early
efforts, John Aspinall began to campaign for the return of this species
to China during the 1990s.

As a result, in November 1992, ten horses (comprising five stallions and five mares) were sent by TAF to the Milu Ecological Centre near Beijing, China with a view to eventually releasing them into the Gansu Nature Reserve. One mare was also sent to the Hustain Nuruu Steppe Reserve in Mongolia in 1996 as part of a collaborative reintroduction project that had been established two years previously.

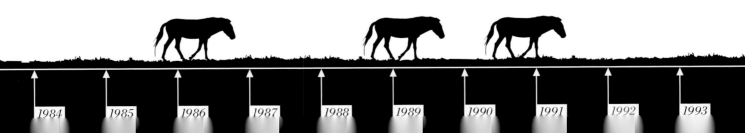

1984   1985   1986   1987   1988   1989   1990   1991   1992   1993

1993

TAF's work at the gorilla orphanage in Brazzaville, Congo proved to be so successful that it was forced to undergo a rapid expansion, leading eventually to the establishment of the Lésio-Louna gorilla sanctuary, adjacent to the Lefini Wildlife Reserve, in April 1993. Other primates, predominantly bonobos, were also taken in and repatriated, including Max, who was eventually rehomed at the Lola ya Bonobo sanctuary in neighbouring DRC in 2004.

(Right) Although the Sumatran rhino project ran into initial obstacles, the scheme involving critically endangered eastern black rhinos soon began to yield dividends. So much so, that by 1995, TAF was able to send a male to join a semi-wild breeding programme at Addo National Park, South Africa. He has since sired at least three calves.

1995

1996

Three years after the Congo gorilla rehabilitation project moved to its new home, the first six rescued gorillas were released into the Lesio-Louna Reserve. Although the scheme received an annual average of 10+ orphans during the early years, joint efforts with local government to raise awareness and enforce legal restrictions meant that this number began to drop considerably after 1998.

Nearly 80% of the animals currently held in captivity are not rare or endangered.

Damian Aspinall believes that in the future, zoos and wildlife parks should be looking to keep and breed only those animal species that are threatened or endangered, and then only as part of a reintroduction programme.

For him, keeping animals locked up, often in conditions far removed from what they would enjoy in the wild, is a cultural misconception and a bit akin to slavery - something that we will one day look back upon with shame.

Sadly, despite TAF's best efforts to breed with Torgamba, the programme reached a dead end. So, in 1998, Torgamba was transferred to an onsite breeding programme in Sumatra where attempts to mate him continue. Nevertheless, the captive-breeding programme initiated by The Aspinall Foundation did eventually yield results, albeit indirectly: several American zoos took up the challenge from 1987, finally resulting in a birth in 2001 at Cincinnati Zoo.

Also in 1998, seven more gorillas were released from the African gorilla sanctuary.

So successful was the Congo-based western lowland gorilla rescue and reintroduction programme that it was expanded to the neighbouring Republic of Gabon in 1998.

1999

TAF's aim to release animals from their UK captive breeding programmes became a reality in 1999 when two male captive-born gorillas from Kent were repatriated to Gabon.

Combined, the two gorilla projects in Africa cover almost 1 million acres of pristine forest and savannah within the unique ecosystem of the Batéké Plateau that spans Gabon and the Congo. This region is generally considered to be a biodiversity hotspot where species such as forest elephants, red river hog and forest buffalo also roam freely. TAF's conservation efforts in Africa therefore extend across a much wider species range than just the gorillas that it releases here.

The first 17 gorillas were released in Gabon, including Kwam, the first
Howletts-born gorilla ever to be released into the wild; with nine more
gorilla orphans being released in Congo the same year.

2002

The Batéké Plateau National Park was created in Gabon, incorporating the TAF gorilla reintroduction site. The charity also worked with the IUCN on developing guidelines for primate reintroductions, which were published in 2002, followed by similar advice for great apes in 2007.

A group of seven gorillas, led by Kwibi, left Kent for reintroduction in Gabon.

2004

Téké, born in the Congo reserve in April 2004, was the first infant
born to reintroduced gorillas anywhere in the world. He celebrated his
10th birthday in the same month as TAF's 30th anniversary.

Téké's birth was followed by four more in Congo in 2006, with the first reintroduced gorilla birth in the Gabon occurring in 2007. By the end of 2013, over 25 births had been recorded across the two TAF-run projects.

Thanks to TAF's successful captive breeding programmes in Kent, the charity was also able to send a clouded leopard pair to Cambodia in 2006 to bolster a local captive breeding programme.

2007

TAF's conservation programmes in Africa do much more than just reintroduce gorillas – they also help to restore and conserve close to a million acres of savannah and rain forest, whose fragile eco-systems have been upset by destructive practices such as deforestation, bush fires and poaching. Other fauna that indirectly benefit from TAF's work in the national parks in the Congo and Gabon include elephants, leopards, small antelope and rodents.

In 2007, a male and female rhino from Port Lympne Reserve were transferred to the Tanzanian Serengeti. The move was a part of a pioneering partnership between TAF, the Tanzanian government and a private reserve based within the Serengeti National Park. These were the first ever captive-born rhinos to be reintroduced into the area.

In 2008, TAF expanded its overseas projects by establishing a lemur conservation programme in Madagascar. Focussed primarily on saving the critically endangered greater bamboo lemur, the programme developed several participatory and community-based conservation activities that eventually helped remove this shy and beautiful creature from the list of the 25 most endangered primates in the world.

2008

Although TAF's African projects initially led to a reduction in wildlife crimes in the region, a mini resurgence in ivory trafficking in 2006, together with an increase in primate orphan numbers due to poaching, suggested the need for reinforcement. As a result, TAF teamed up with the Congolese authorities and several wildlife organisations in 2008 to form PALF, a collaborative initiative aimed at reducing poaching and illegal wildlife trade.

Over the years, PALF's efforts have resulted in several significant seizures of live animals, animal pelts and other animal products, including the confiscation of a large stash of ivory and multiple arrests in one of Brazzaville's biggest ivory trafficking networks.

The group has also been responsible for bringing to justice over 250 offenders, including some corrupt Ecoguards, members of a militia group involved in poaching, and a Chinese national, who was sentenced to four years in prison for ivory trafficking. In several court cases, the maximum sentence for a wildlife criminal – five years in prison – was handed out – a phenomenon that is slowly becoming more commonplace.

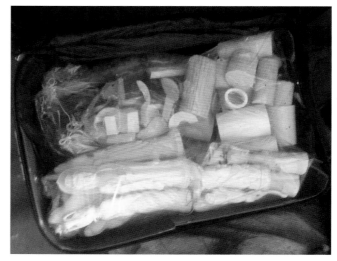

The gorilla projects model was later replicated in Indonesia, with the creation, in December 2009, of a Javan primate conservation programme. Known as The Cry of the Wild, the project led to the creation of two rescue and rehabilitation centres in east and west Java to help save and protect Javan langurs and gibbons from threats such as loss of habitat, the illegal wildlife trade and hunting. Both centres are surrounded by large areas of protected forest, helping to conserve the rapidly dwindling natural habitat for these animals and preserving it for other native flora and fauna.

TAF's overseas efforts in Madagascar included three years of collaborative species surveys, conducted with the help of local communities. These proved to be groundbreaking, resulting in the discovery of several new populations of the greater bamboo lemur. Not only did this double the number of known lemur habitation sites in the wild, but it also led to the removal of this species from the list of the 25 most endangered primates in the world, for the first time in a decade.

2010

In a bid to unobtrusively monitor the welfare of newly reintroduced animals, as well as gather more scientific data about the wildlife inhabiting its conservation sites, TAF decided to introduce camera traps to a number of its overseas projects, beginning with TAF's Indonesian projects in 2010.

This was later expanded in 2011 to the charity's African programmes where they have helped to keep track of newly reintroduced gorilla groups, identifying new births whilst simultaneously gaining valuable insights into the health of other species within the parks, such as leopards, which are very reclusive by nature.

In June 2011, the first six Javan gibbons, including a wild born male named Aom, and two captive-born gibbons, Cheri and Ukong, were rescued from terrible conditions within the illegal pet trade, and taken to the Javan primate centre for rehabilitation. The charity's breeding programme with this species, which begun to yield results as early as 1988, has enjoyed incredible breeding successes– currently, 90% of all Javan gibbons born in captivity in the UK are born at one of TAF's two managed parks.

In the same year, a new project was started in Madagascar to save the critically endangered black-and-white ruffed lemur, which are ongoing victims of deforestation, hunting and trapping. These included more thorough population surveys and habitat conservation efforts in conjunction with collaborative captive breeding programmes in Europe and North America.

2012

The first captive birth is celebrated in Java. September 2012 also marked the first release of 13 Javan ebony langurs at TAF's project in the country.

The 25th birth is celebrated for the African gorilla project.

Three more black rhinos, Grumeti, Zawadi and Monduli, left Kent for reintroduction to Tanzania.

Thanks to improved populations surveys carried out by the TAF Madagascar team, the greater bamboo lemur was removed from the list of the 25 most endangered primates in the world list.

Djala and his family of nine are sent to Gorilla Island in Gabon for release in 2014.

Five langurs and one gibbon were returned to Java from Kent.

In the UK, TAF played an instrumental role in the development of a conservation action plan to save the critically endangered Scottish wildcat.

2014

In May 2014 ,TAF's Java Primate Rescue Centre released six Javan langurs, two of whom had come from Port Lympne Reserve. After spending time at the primate centre acclimatising to their new life, they have now been released into a protected area in Java.

Working in collaboration with four animal parks in the UK and Ireland, six European bison were successfully translocated to the wild in Romania as part of conservation efforts to bring back Europe's largest land mammal from extinction in the wild.

Oudiki and Kouki in 2014 after six years in Africa.

In May 2014 , The Aspinall Foundation Java Primate Rescue Centre released a family of Javan gibbons into a protected area. Ukong and Cheri were the first to be rescued by the primate centre; they later had a baby named Uchi and have now become the first gibbons TAF has released into the wild.

Building on its successes in Africa, Madagascar and Java, TAF plans to continue the fight for the conservation of wildlife through reintroduction, protection and awareness programmes.

2005   2006   2007   2008   2009   2010   2011   2012   2013   *2014*

"There is a very obvious rationale behind breeding animals. We don't breed them for our curiosity or for medical knowledge or anything like that, but purely to conserve them in a group in as natural conditions as possible, so that one day in the future they can be put back."

JOHN ASPINALL

Djala's journey

Ever wondered why the image of a gorilla adorns the logo of The Aspinall Foundation? Since its inception, the charity has enjoyed unprecedented breeding and reintroduction successes with this particular primate species, with over 130 births and 60+ gorillas released back into the wild – more than any other organisation in the world. But every success story has to start somewhere and in this case, the tale begins with the plight of a male western lowland gorilla named Djala.

Born in the Congolese rainforests near a village called Djala, he was just a baby when his family group was captured by poachers and slaughtered for bush meat. Unlike his unfortunate kin, Djala was rescued by a French mineral prospector who bartered for his release and took him to Brazzaville, where he was put into the care of Yvette Leroy, a French expatriate who looked after him until his growing strength and complex needs meant he needed more specialist care. By chance, Yvette happened to see a documentary about the work of John Aspinall on television, and in 1986, Djala was donated to Howletts where he was lovingly rehabilitated.

Moved by the plight of gorillas like Djala, John Aspinall set up a TAF-run gorilla sanctuary in the Congo in 1987 as a local safe haven for any future orphaned primates. Initially, the Congo gorilla protection project consisted of an orphanage and rehabilitation centre, set within the confines of Brazzaville Zoo and later, the Lésio-Louna Reserve. However, the Congo project was so successful that it was later extended into neighbouring Gabon in 1998, in an area which ultimately became the Batéke Plateau National Park.

Despite arriving in Kent as a traumatised youth with arthritic knees and a broken heart, under the care of the Aspinalls and their team, Djala soon grew into a healthy, well-adjusted male silverback, eventually becoming head of his own gorilla band at the Palace of the Apes at Port Lympne Reserve. However, because of his earlier experiences, Djala was never entirely comfortable with the presence of humans.

In 2012, Damian Aspinall, now Chairman of TAF, decided that the right thing to do was repatriate Djala and his family back to their ancestral homelands. And so, on the 23rd of June 2013, with the aid of DHL, he and nine of his wives and children began their 3000 mile journey from Kent to the jungles of Africa. You can see a step-by-step photo story of his journey in the pages that follow, including Djala's 'Walk to Freedom' from Gorilla Island in June 2014, after he and his family had spent a year acclimatising to their new home in Gabon.

In essence then, Djala's story embodies what The Aspinall Foundation is all about: the successful rescue, rehabilitation, and eventual repatriation of endangered wild animal species back to their native environments.

Djala and his family at Port Lympne Reserve.

Each gorilla has a full medical check to prepare them for the long journey.

Gorilla keeper, Helen, keeps Djala company as he travels to the transporter.

The gorillas are loaded in their individual crates into the DHL truck that will take them on the first stage of their journey back to the wild.

Damian Aspinall, Chairman of
The Aspinall Foundation oversees
each stage of the gorillas' move.

Djala and his family start their journey
back to the wild made possible with
the support of DHL.

The crates used to house Djala and all nine of his family members during their
trip back to Africa were tailor-made to fit the dimensions of each individual
gorilla by DHL. The logistics company partnered with The Aspinall Foundation
in transporting the gorillas, along with food and vet equipment weighing some
1200 kg, from Kent to Gabon. DHL are no strangers to this sort of special
delivery – in 2012, they also generously assisted with the transfer of three
endangered black rhinos from Port Lympne Reserve to Tanzania where they
were released from captivity in the hopes of repopulating the region.

Djala and his family are loaded into the plane ready for the
next stage of their journey.

The gorillas get the first glimpse of their ancestral homeland when they are unloaded at the airport in Gabon, Africa.

Djala is transported by boat across to the
island where he started his life in Africa.

The Aspinall Foundation's 'Back to the Wild' programme is the only one of
its kind in the world to successfully breed, rehabilitate and then reintroduce
western lowland gorillas. No other wildlife conservation organisation
currently has the experience and will to do this kind of work. Not only
is it very expensive, but the process is painstaking and can take years to
complete. However, Damian Aspinall believes that if you are going to do
something, you should do so wholeheartedly and without thought for cost.
For him, the animals deserve nothing less.

Each gorilla is unloaded from the boat onto a release platform.

The crates are opened and the gorillas take their first steps on African soil to explore a whole new world.

Djala settled quickly into life on the island where he was to spend the next year.

Akou – the youngest member of Djala's group adapted quickly and is happy up in the trees.

Djala is safely on Gorilla Island and starts to explore what will be his home for the next year while he and his family habituate.

Djala is protective of the females in his group who stay close to him.

In June 2014, the bridge from Gorilla Island was put into position, and the gorillas made the crossing over the Mpassa River and into the Bateke Plateau National Park, where they are now free to roam. Djala and Kibi can be seen here taking their first steps onto the bridge.

Although they have initially returned to the sanctuary of Gorilla Island each night since their release, it is hoped they will eventually feel safe enough to remain in the rain forests and integrate fully into the local environment.

Djala walking across the bridge from Gorilla Island to protected reserve.

Akou, the youngest member of Djala's group making the journey across into the reserve.

Djala back in the wild where he belongs.

"Traditional conservationists might say that The Aspinall Foundation had done its job in rescuing Djala…BUT I passionately believe they would be wrong. I do not believe that keeping and breeding animals in captivity can or should be the end game of conservation in the 21st Century. That end game, I believe, has to be, wherever possible, the safe return of these wonderful animals to their ancestral homelands, to the wild where nature meant them to live."

DAMIAN ASPINALL

the next chapter

John Aspinall's dream in founding The Aspinall Foundation (TAF) in 1984 was to find a way to protect, breed and return wild animals to their natural habitats. Thanks to his unswerving dedication and the determination of his successors, this dream has become a reality. Having slowly integrated TAF's two parks, Howletts and Port Lympne, with TAF's overseas projects, they now form a kind of mini ecosystem in which the charity can carry out the backbone of its work: the rehabilitation and, ultimately, reintroduction of rare and endangered species.

Undoubtedly, TAF's greatest success to date is its gorilla reintroduction programme. John Aspinall's unorthodox but compassionate approach to animal husbandry has resulted in the births of over 135 gorilla babies since 1957, while in Africa, the 'Back to the Wild' programme has helped to complete the bookend by successfully reintroducing more than 60 gorillas back to their natural habitat.

Although charity chairman, Damian Aspinall, is really proud of TAF's breeding records, which continue to outstrip those of most other zoological institutions in the world, he doesn't plan to let the organisation rest on its laurels. Just as the species in his care have been doing for millions of years, he feels the charity needs to adapt to current conditions.

"We're constantly evolving, which is what I think you have to do - we don't want to become a stamp collection."

Damian is keenly aware that deforestation, land development, poaching and illegal trafficking in wildlife products are bringing many animals closer and closer to the brink of extinction, so more needs to be done to preserve them, as well as the natural environments in which they live, for future generations. Already, TAF's overseas conservation projects are leading the way in this regard. In Africa, they work closely with the governments of Congo and Gabon to combat crimes such as poaching, wildlife trafficking, and illegal logging; and to increase the number of protected sites in the region so that indigenous flora and fauna populations can recover from environmental degradation.

In keeping with the views of his father, Damian also feels that zoos need to make a concerted effort to reorganise their collections to reflect the extinction threat facing many species - currently, only about 75-80% of the animals kept in zoos are rare or endangered - something he feels needs to change.

"The whole question of zoos needs to be looked at. They should probably be phased out in 20 years."

In the interim, as long as there is a need for wildlife sanctuaries such as Howletts and Port Lympne, Damian will continue to keep them open. John Aspinall believed that the fundamental aim of zoos and wildlife parks should be to breed and ultimately return endangered wild animals back to their natural environments, and TAF's philosophy remains firmly rooted in this position.

Going forward into the 21st century, the focus for The Aspinall Foundation will become increasingly about a joined-up approach to environmental conservation and species reintroduction. These aims can only be achieved by expanding the charity's overseas wildlife rehabilitation and reintroduction projects, using its gorilla programme as a model, and in tandem with this, continuing to build on its efforts to restore, preserve and protect whole ecosystems for posterity.

As an example, TAF is currently in talks with the National Parks authorities in Gabon about the possibility of increasing the types of species that could be reintroduced within their reserves, with the long term aim of bringing back locally extinct species such as waterbuck, reedbuck, hippo, lion and hunting dog.

In order to do this kind of work sustainably, a holistic approach to conservation is essential. In real terms, this often means undertaking ecosystem restoration, as well as creating community engagement and development programmes to run in tandem with TAF's species reintroduction schemes, as a way of safeguarding the long term success of their projects as a whole.

The charity has also gone to great lengths to develop alternative, more sustainable sources of employment and income for the communities living near to its wildlife projects. For example, in Madagascar, currently one of the world's poorest nations, TAF has enlisted the help of local community associations (COBAs) to help manage its lemur conservation areas, as well as conduct educational programmes and carry out locally-led wildlife surveys. Already this programme has

generated much-needed economic benefits for local people whilst providing vital information to the scientific community about several of the most highly threatened primate species in the wild, all the while saving several greater bamboo lemur populations from imminent extinction.

Combined, these efforts help to ensure that TAF's conservation programmes end up protecting so much more than just one species within a particular ecosystem. All of this is a painstakingly slow and expensive endeavour, but one that the Aspinall family feels is extremely worthwhile, especially given how much is at stake for the future of our planet.

In the words of the late John Aspinall:

"I believe that wilderness is Earth's greatest treasure. Wilderness is the bank on which all cheques are drawn. I believe our debt to nature is total; our willingness to pay anything back on account, barely discernible. I believe that, unless we recognise this debt and renegotiate it, we write our own epitaph."

"We are in the business of conservation not the conservation of business."

DAMIAN ASPINALL

Having brought the vision of his father full circle, Damian Aspinall believes that in the future, zoos should only exist to help conserve and breed endangered creatures, rather than focusing on making money or entertaining humans, especially if this comes at the expense of animal welfare. He looks forward to the day when his two wildlife parks become redundant and will continue to change the make-up of the collections at Howletts and Port Lympne so that they remain, first and foremost, breeding sanctuaries for animals that can be reintroduced.

Dave Rolfe

Born in Folkestone, Kent, Dave Rolfe took up photography as a hobby during his early adult years, and spent his spare time honing his craft in between running a local family business with his wife, Bev. Always mad about wildlife, he did a bird ringing course at Dungeness, a hotspot for many species of migrating birds, as a young man. He still takes a keen interest in bird photography, and his pictures have been exhibited by the Wild Fowl Trust in Norfolk, amongst other places.

Dave has been a part of the TAF family since 1987 when he entered a photographic exhibition at Howletts. His pictures so impressed the late John Aspinall that he commissioned Dave then and there to take some photographs of the animals at his wildlife parks. Ever since that day, Dave has never looked back. As one of the Official Photographers for The Aspinall Foundation (TAF), he has spent the last three decades documenting the charity's highs and lows. From record-breaking births to anniversaries and organisational milestones, Dave has seen and photographed it all. It should come as no surprise then, that he has managed to build up quite an extensive photographic archive of the charity's history, and it is mainly his work that you see in the pages of this book.

In addition to this commemorative publication, which Dave sees as his way of repaying John Aspinall for giving him his big break all those years ago, Dave's wildlife photographs have also been published in National Geographic, Time Life, as well as many local UK newspapers and magazines.

Now semi-retired, he regularly travels to places such as Germany, Africa and North America to capture wild creatures in their natural settings, from black bears in the forests of Minnesota to the herds of wildebeest that roam the plains of the Masai Mara in Kenya.

Dave also regularly runs wildlife photographic courses at Port Lympne Reserve and Howletts Wild Animal Park. From small group workshops to one-to-one tuition, Dave enjoys helping aspiring photographers get up close and personal with the animals and teaching them how to capture those memorable 'one-off' shots that every snapper dreams about.

You can find out more about his work by visiting:
www.wildlife-shots.co.uk.

Lisa Mendes

A Kent-based writer and editor, Lisa Mendes grew up in South Africa where she developed a love of nature and an interest in conservation.

After studying journalism at Rhodes University, she worked within the South African broadcasting and film industries, including several high profile current affairs programmes and an award-winning documentary, before moving to the UK in 2001.

Since then, she has become more involved in writing and publishing, working for a well-known newspaper group and later, as a copywriter, for a PR firm, before going freelance in 2011.

Prior to this book, which she very much considers to be a labour of love, Lisa edited a non-fiction reference publication for the Urania Trust. In between freelancing for a number of private clients and publishing houses in London, she is working on a non-fiction book, which she hopes to finish as soon as time allows.

You can find out more about her at: www.lisamendes.co.uk

John Devlin

Originally a native of Essex, John, left his employment in the record industry in 1998 to study Graphic Design in Maidstone, Kent. Since earning his degree he settled in the county permanently and has forged a successful career in design. Today he runs The Design Practice, a graphic design agency who in 2014 celebrate their 20th anniversary, for more information visit www.thedesignpractice.co.uk

Outside of his design career John is an internationally published author with two volumes of his history of football kit design, 'True Colours', under his belt. Now seen as one of the country's experts on the subject, John regularly writes and illustrates for various magazines and books as well as commenting on football kit matters for radio.

John has also designed and published two photographic books on the local history of the village where he lives.

He is married with one daughter.

Photo Credits

All photos © David Rolfe except: © Getty Images: page 9 (top) & pages 44-45 / © Nick Nichols: page 38 / © Dmitri Kasterine: page 49 /
© Aspinall Family: pages 25, 27, 30, 31, 37 & 39 / © Tony King: pages 127, 137, 138, 139, 145 (right) & 146 (left) /
© Hery Randriahaingo: page 121 bottom left) / © Martin Dallimer: page 132 / © Elke Boyen & Sander Muilerman: page 135 / © Paul Aczel: page 140 (left) /
© Maholy Ravaloharimanitra: page 141 / © Tiana Ratolojanahary: page 143 (bottom) / © Bryan Curran: page 147 (top left) /
© Various including Derek Betts & Matthieu Bonnet: pages 152-169 / Images on pages 66, 68-69, 70, 75, 76, 77 taken from Country Life.

CHANGE FOR CONSERVATION

We hope that you have enjoyed your journey with us through the TAF archives. Perhaps, now that you've gotten to know more about our unique philosophy and the important work that we do for conservation, you might consider making a donation to support The Aspinall Foundation's overseas animal protection projects.

The Aspinall Foundation is the charity that works with Howletts Wild Animal Park and Port Lympne Reserve.
The Aspinall Foundation runs wildlife conservation projects in Congo, Gabon, Madagascar and Java. It has returned more animals to the wild than any other organisation in the world.

THE ASPINALL
FOUNDATION
REGISTERED CHARITY NO. 326567

YOUR DONATION COULD HELP PROTECT A SPECIES:

£10 could buy bedding for the crates we use when returning animals to the wild

£15 could buy dried milk, used to supplement the diets of young gorillas returned to the wild

£25 could help plant trees, buy bamboo and matting which is used for enrichment, nourishment and shading at the Java Primate Rescue Centre

£50 could help purchase tents, sleeping bags and radio handsets used by our overseas staff on poaching patrols

Pennies make pounds!
All donations make a difference.

I enclose a gift of £ .... To support THE ASPINALL FOUNDATION'S vital work.

Please give us your details

Name...

Address...

....

Postcode..

For individuals:

giftaid it ☐ **YES,** I am a UK tax payer* and I wish THE ASPINALL FOUNDATION to claim Gift Aid on all donations I have made for four years prior to this year, and on all donations I have made from the date of this declaration until I notify you otherwise.
☐ Please tick if you are not a **UK taxpayer.**

Today's Date ....

*To qualify for Gift Aid, you must pay an amount of UK Income Tax and/or Capital Gains Tax at least equal to the tax that The Aspinall Foundaton reclaims on your donations in the appropriate tax year (currently 25p for each £1 given)

Please fill in your payment details
Here is my gift of £.........................

☐ I enclose a cheque/CAF voucher payable to: **The Aspinall Foundation**
☐ I would like to pay by Mastercard/Visa/CAF card/Switch/Delta
(delete as appropriate)

Card Number ☐☐☐☐ ☐☐☐☐ ☐☐☐☐ ☐☐☐☐
Valid from ☐☐/☐☐ Expiry date ☐☐/☐☐
Issue number (Switch/Delta only) ☐☐ Security Code ☐☐☐
(Last 3 numbers on your signature strip)
Signature...Date....................

☐ I would like to receive regular updates from THE ASPINALL FOUNDATION by email

....

If you would like to speak to a member of THE ASPINALL FOUNDATION's Supporter Care Team please call us on 01303 234 199 (Mon-Fri 9am to 5pm)

Registered Charity no. 326567   **Charity address is The Aspinall Foundation, FREEPOST RLUL-CXBS-SHGL, Aldington Road, Lympne, Hythe, Kent, CT21 4PD**

Visit www.aspinallfoundation.org for more about the charity.